# The Effective

# SUPERVISORY MANAGEMENT

### NVQ Level 3

*Managing People:*
*Successful Teams*

PITMAN PUBLISHING
128 Long Acre, London WC2E 9AN

© Institute of Management 1995
Prepared by Steve Morris and Graham Willcocks in association with
the Institute of Management

*British Library Cataloguing in Publication Data*
A CIP catalogue record for this book is available
on request from the British Library.

ISBN 0-273-61534-3

All rights reserved. No part of this publication may be
reproduced, stored in a retrieval system, or transmitted
in any form or by any means, electronic, mechanical,
photocopying, recording, or otherwise without either the
prior written permission of the Publisher. This book
may not be lent, resold, hired out or otherwise disposed
of by way of trade in any form of binding or cover other than that
in which it is published, without the prior consent of the Publisher.

10 9 8 7 6 5 4 3 2 1

Typeset by Technolyne
Printed and bound in Great Britain
by Hobbs the Printers, Totton, Hampshire SO40 3YS

# Contents

**Before you start** — 3
   The level of learning — 3
   Evidence collection — 4

**Workpacks in this series** — 5

**Links to the MCI Standards** — 6

**Introduction** — 8

**Objectives** — 9

## Section 1
### WHAT TEAMS ARE AND WHY THEY MATTER — 11
   Why teams are special — 13
   Why have teams? — 17

## Section 2
### WHAT MAKES EFFECTIVE TEAMS? — 27
   The conditions needed for effective teams — 29
   The right mix of skills — 33

## Section 3
### YOUR ROLE AS TEAM LEADER — 51
   The three circles — 52
   Who is the team leader? — 56
   Personal qualities - communication, openness and trust — 57

## Section 4
### DEVELOPING THE TEAM — 61
   Planning team development — 63
   Stages in the development of a team — 63
   Determining the priorities — 68
   Planning the action — 73
   Implementation and reviewing action — 77

| | |
|---|---:|
| Summary | 81 |
| Recommended reading | 83 |
| About the audio cassettes | 85 |
| About the Institute of Management | 87 |
| Ordering information | 89 |

# Before you start

In each of the workbooks in this series you will find this same preface. It is here to give you a clear picture of the common aspects of the series and the links between this workbook and your overall competence. It is here to help you get the most from the work you put in.

## The level of learning

This workbook is designed at a level that covers each of the elements in the Management Charter Initiative (MCI) Standards for Supervisors. However, it doesn't stop there, for two reasons:

1. Learning and development is as much about the future as it is about the here and now. It is important that you have all the information to cover the knowledge and understanding needed for the supervisory standards – but you deserve to have insight into what more senior managers do. You may be one yourself in the future and starting any new job is more productive if you do not have to start learning everything from scratch.

2. No supervisor or manager works in isolation – you saw this in the Foundation Module. To get the most from your work it helps immensely if you can see it in context, the context of the role other managers and specialists play as they work alongside you. If you know where your part of the process fits in with everyone else's then it makes the picture more recognisable and more satisfying.

So don't worry when you read about some topics that don't form part of your direct role at the moment – or are asked to carry out some activities at that level. It's meant to be this way.

You will find that many of the activities ask you to look - as a supervisor - at your organisation, and investigate or explore issues. This is straightforward enough if you are already a supervisor and it is an essential link if you are collecting evidence for MCI qualifications.

However, where the activities ask you to think, the fact you are not yet a supervisor will make little difference - and this is the case in most activities. If you feel there are places where the need for specific information or documents means it is important to look at the activity from a supervisory perspective, though, do not worry.

You can still:

- look at your organisation from your own experience, even though it is not yet as a supervisor, and ask to see documents you might otherwise ignore or not be given - many are not confidential, they just are not given to everyone because they are not relevant to them in their current role

- find a colleague who is a supervisor who can talk some of the issues through with you, show you any documents and help you where the activities really need a supervisory input

- identify another organisation that you know - maybe one you have worked in, or one where a close friend works and - with the appropriate degree of respect, permission and confidentiality - use it as the basis for your analysis and thought.

## Evidence collection

The evidence requirements for a qualification under MCI guidelines are in two parts. The first says consistently that you need to demonstrate your competence through... 'performance at work over a period of time'.

Clearly no workbook can do this for you because it means you need to gather the evidence from your own activities, not from a theoretical source - however relevant and helpful that source is. However it can help you by giving pointers to let you think through what makes up effective performance.

# Workpacks in this series

Each workpack consists of a workbook and an audio cassette (with the exception of the foundation module). The workpacks and cassettes can be ordered individually.

The titles in the series are grouped into four key areas:

**Foundation Module**
**Managing People**
- The Recruitment and Selection Process
- Leading from the Middle
- Successful Teams
- Effective Interviewing
- Managing Yourself
- Mastering Supervision and Appraisal
- Effective Delegation
- Health and Safety
- Developing People
- Getting the Best from People
- Personnel Management
- Handling Difficult Situations and People

**Managing Information**
- Effective Communication
- Managing Information
- Getting the Message Over
- Running Effective Meetings

**Managing Finance**
- Finance Made Easy
- Contributing to Budgetary Control

**Managing Products and services**
- Managing Operations
- Quality Management
- Handling Change
- Managing Projects

You will find ordering information at the back of this book.

# Links to the MCI Standards

In the following matrix, titles in normal type are core workbooks for the MCI Units shown. Where titles also relate to other workbooks – as well as those with core links - they are shown again in italics.

| **Foundation Module** |
|---|
| This sets the scene for the rest of the series, and looks at the role and responsibilities of the supervisor, the background to organisations where supervisors work, and ways to get the most from open learning. |

| **MCI Units and Elements** | **Workbooks** |
|---|---|
| **Unit 1 Maintain Services and Operations to Meet Quality Standards** <br> **Elements** <br> 1.1 Maintain Services and Operations <br> 1.2 Maintain the Necessary Conditions for an Effective and Safe Work Environment | Managing Operations <br> Quality Management <br> Handling Change <br> Health and Safety |
| **Unit 2 Contribute to Planning, Monitoring and Control of Resources** <br> **Elements** <br> 2.1 Plan for the Use of Resources <br> 2.2 Monitor and Control the Use of Resources | Finance Made Easy <br><br> Contributing to Budgetary Control |
| **Unit 3 Contribute to the Provision of Personnel** <br> **Elements** <br> 3.1 Contribute to the Identification of Personnel Requirements <br> 3.2 Contribute to the Selection of Personnel | The Recruitment and Selection Process <br><br> *Effective Interviewing* |
| **Unit 4 Contribute to the Training and Development of Teams, Individuals and Self to Enhance Performance** <br> **Elements** <br> 4.1 Contribute to Planning the Training and Development of Teams and Individuals <br> 4.2 Contribute to Training and Development Activities for Teams and Individuals <br> 4.3 Contribute to the Assessment of Teams and Individuals Against Training and Development Objectives <br> 4.4 Develop Oneself Within the Job | Successful Teams <br> Developing People <br> Managing Yourself <br> *Mastering Supervision and Appraisal* <br><br> *Effective Delegation* |

| MCI Units and Elements | Workbooks |
|---|---|
| **Unit 5 Contribute to the Planning, Organisation and Evaluation of Work**<br>**Elements**<br>5.1 Contribute to Planning Work Activities and Methods to Achieve Objectives<br>5.2 Organise Work and Assist in the Evaluation of Work<br>5.3 Provide Feedback on Work Performance to Teams and Individuals | Mastering Supervision and Appraisal<br>Supervising for Results<br>Effective Delegation<br>Managing Projects |
| **Unit 6 Create, Maintain and Enhance Productive Working Relationships**<br>**Elements**<br>6.1 Create and Enhance Productive Working Relationships With Colleagues and Those for Whom One has Supervisory Responsibility<br>6.2 Enhance Productive Working Relationship with One's Immediate Manager<br>6.3 Identify and Minimise Interpersonal Conflict<br>6.4 Contribute to the Implementation of Disciplinary and Grievance Procedures | Leading from the Middle<br>Effective Delegation<br>Getting the Best from People<br>Personnel Management<br>Effective Interviewing<br>Handling Difficult Situations and People |
| **Unit 7 Provide Information and Advice for Action Towards Meeting Organisational Objectives**<br>**Elements**<br>7.1 Obtain, Evaluate, Record and Store Information<br>7.2 Provide Information and Advice<br>    Effective Communication | Effective Communication<br>Getting the Message Over<br>Running Effective Meetings<br>Managing Information |

# Introduction

Teams are a common issue and topic of conversation in management and supervisor circles these days. Organisations everywhere seem to be looking at developing a more team-based approach – and that means getting everyone involved.

You will know that you are in several teams all at the same time – some you lead, others are led by someone else. The problem is that just calling a group of people a team doesn't make it a team. There are specific characteristics that distinguish real teams from the rest.

These characteristics need developing to make them come alive – in the same way as the leader of a sports team has to do. Just selecting the right number of people who will turn up on a given day doesn't mean they will perform as a team. There are subtle and clear qualities that make a team effective. They aren't always easy to achieve… but then the best things often aren't.

This workbook looks at why teams matter to you, the people in the teams and the organisation. It also explores the qualities needed for a really effective team and how you can increase its performance through planned development. There are issues like:

- **the roles people need to play to get a balanced team**
- **the style of communication**
- **the way people treat each other**
- **the role of the person leading the team.**

In some particular units and elements of the MCI Standards the emphasis is on developing and training teams. So, in this workbook there is a natural focus on the role you play at the head of your teams at work. But teams are at work all the time – effective teamwork is a positive factor in your success in most if not all the MCI Standards, even the most unlikely. You can't control budgets, manage projects or run operations without some degree of teamwork, for instance.

This workbook helps you develop teams so that you can get better results and derive more satisfaction from your role as a supervisor leading a team.

# Objectives

By the end of this workbook you will be able to:

- explain the benefits of effective teams for the individual, the organisation and the supervisor
- describe the characteristics of well-developed teams
- assess the strengths and weaknesses of teams against criteria for success
- determine objectives for developing the team
- gain support and involvement from the team in their own development
- use techniques that will help build, maintain and develop a team approach
- relate the above objectives to your own organisation, your own role and progress towards meeting MCI standards.

Meeting these objectives will allow you to develop knowledge and understanding towards the following parts of the MCI Standards, in particular the following Elements of Unit 4.

---

**Unit 4  Contribute to the training and development of teams, individuals and self to enhance performance**

**Elements**

4.1   Contribute to Planning the Training and Development of Teams and Individuals

4.2   Contribute to Training and Development Activities for Teams and Individuals

4.3   Contribute to the Assessment of Teams and Individuals Against Training and Development Objectives

---

It also relates to elements in other Units, especially:

---

5.2   Organise Work and Assist in Evaluation of Work

6.1   Create and Enhance Productive Working Relationships With Colleagues and Those for Whom One has Supervisory Responsibility

---

SECTION

# WHAT TEAMS ARE AND WHY THEY MATTER

*'We trained hard... but it seemed that every time we were beginning to form up into teams we would be reorganised. I was to learn later in life that we tend to meet any new situation by reorganising, and a wonderful method it can be for creating the illusion of progress while producing confusion, inefficiency and demoralisation.'*

Petronius Arbiter 270 BC

In other words, just saying you are forming a team doesn't mean much. It can work against you unless you think it through and work hard at building, developing and maintaining an effective team.

Real teams are special and they need special treatment and development. A consultant specialising in team development tells the following story.

### The Management Team

'I worked with an organisation's management team on a quality initiative. It was fascinating. They called themselves the 'management team' but I've never seen anything less like a team in my life.

The Chief Executive was weak and let the others do what they thought best, even if it meant doing entirely different things in different departments. The other members were all heads of department – and that's the role they brought into the team. They never worked together for the benefit of the organisation. Instead they fought their own corner, picked each other off and played power games inside and outside their meetings.

They asked me what they ought to do. My first comment was to stop calling themselves a Management Team and start calling themselves a Heads of Department Meeting before someone sued them under the Trade Descriptions legislation. There is more than a subtle difference in the names.'

Graham Thomas, Wesley House Consultants.

## Why teams are special

When two or more people come together in any circumstances you could end up with all sorts of gatherings, such as:

- a work group
- a Heads of Department Meeting
- a crowd
- a committee
- a team.

They are not all the same and this gives a clue to why teams are special.

It is important to work out exactly what makes a team different from other sorts of gatherings and groups, before starting to focus on what makes them effective, and what development you can do as a supervisor. If you try and build a team on the wrong foundation it will collapse – like anything else you try and construct.

## Activity 1.1

Write down some examples of teams – any teams – you have seen.

Make some notes about why you think they are teams, rather than other sorts of group.

*This activity may help provide evidence for Unit 4 of the MCI Standards*

## Feedback

One definition of a team is that it is a group of people working together for a common purpose. You've looked at the Heads of Department example, now look at the other sorts of gathering one by one, for a minute.

**A work group** is a number of people who happen to be employed in the same place at the same time. Not all work groups are teams – you may even have noticed examples where individuals seem actively to work against each other, or compete inappropriately. They can become teams, but only if action is taken to make them a team, or they form up against a common enemy.

### Attila the Manager

A County Council officer was describing the section he works in.

*'The boss is awful – he is a complete bully and he never gives any praise. It's always a search for faults, for things to discipline us with. Mind you, at least he's consistent – he hates us all equally.*

*It's even good, in a perverse way. We all get on ever so well together in the face of adversity, covering for each other and helping each other out, so I suppose you could say he's made us into a cracking team.'*

There's no suggestion that you take an approach like this to get your people to form a team. This team is there despite rather than because of the boss. A more positive approach is to work with your people instead of against them. You are, after all, meant to be on the same side.

**A crowd** is generally watching from the outside. It could be a large group who happen to be at the January sales, but everyone is after their own piece of the action – they're all there for their own personal reasons.

Try and get any crowd to move in the same direction and you need mounted police, traffic diversions and people to direct the movement of what is often a faceless mass of bodies.

**A committee** – this must be a team, some would say. But think about it – think about a committee where there are opposing views on an issue. It's not unusual for there to be two or more teams operating within a committee. A contentious issue is discussed, voted on and agreed – but not accepted by those who lost the vote. They leave the meeting and carry on trying to undermine the outcome, working to get the decision reversed. The committee members may be discussing common issues but they are not all after the same result.

*A camel is a horse designed by a committee.*          *Anon.*

Look at it another way. Imagine you are in a bus crossing Dartmoor in the depths of Winter. The people on the bus are all strangers to you and to each other. Suddenly, the bus stops. The driver is ill. It's freezing cold, starting to snow – and no-one has a phone. Then something happens. Within minutes what was a group of strangers either starts to work as a team or, more unlikely, they just sit there.

### Activity 1.2

What are these people likely to do that makes this into a team rather than any other sort of group?

*This activity may help provide evidence for Unit 5 of the MCI Standards*

### Feedback

There are several possibilities and some of the most likely that you wrote down include:

- **there is now a common goal, a common problem that everyone wants to see solved**

- **people start to communicate more, sharing ideas and suggestions, knowledge and information – someone knows where the nearest town is, someone else is experienced in survival techniques, someone knows first aid and looks after the driver and so on**

- **the level of co-operation rises – unless everyone works together each individual will go their own way, or sit there**

- **someone (or some people) probably emerges as a leader and individuals start to assume different tasks, roles and functions within the group, using their own expertise in a collaborative way.**

The team that now exists has a clear purpose and is co-operating to meet it. It will disband once the crisis is over but for now .. it's a team.

But this sort of team formation – almost an accidental team formed by circumstances – is not the usual way. More likely is that you, as a supervisor, will decide to work over a period of time to build a team.

## Why have teams?

There are lots of books about teams, but one question they rarely ask is why have them? Teams may be high on the list of management priorities these days, but why? Could it be that it is just a fad?

The first point to make here is that you don't have to have a team if you don't need one. There are, though, some very good reasons why teams can make a real difference to the success of the individual members and to the organisation as a whole.

Amongst other things, teams:

- **improve the quality of information and decisions, so you have more and better data to help solve problems and implement improvements**
- **help avoid the 'not-invented-here' syndrome, where people reject ideas because they're someone else's and weren't involved in the planning and discussion**
- **are essential in carrying out complicated and complex tasks, so they can be co-ordinated for the benefit of the organisation and its managers**
- **encourage individuals to play a more constructive part in managing their own work, raising motivation, job satisfaction and commitment**
- **help new people to develop a powerful sense of belonging.**

Let's look at each of these in more detail.

### Two heads (or more) are better than one

If there is a simple task with a correct way to do it and an identifiable right answer, fine – give it to one person or do it yourself. If not, a team can add a great deal to the process of reasoning, finding subtle solutions and pooling otherwise disparate information.

Try the following activity, just to prove the point.

### Activity 1.3

Prepare ten questions – factual questions with right and wrong answers – from the procedures and policies where you work. You could collect them from health and safety, discipline, grievance – anything.

Then get together a small group of people – maybe the team you work with.

Give them the questions to answer on their own – no conferring. When they've finished they put those answers to one side – no changing them.

Then get them to come together to share their ideas and arrive at a set of answers they can all live with – they may not all agree exactly but they have to find one common set that is the team response.

Give them the answers and let them mark accurately and fairly their two sets of responses – the individual one and the team's.

Finally, find out which was more accurate – the individual or the team.

*This will help develop skills and understanding relating to Performance Criteria 6.1 (h) and (i) in MCI Standards*

### Feedback

You probably realised that information and decisions are likely to be of better quality if a team is involved. They certainly shouldn't be any worse. As a result team members feel more positive about the eventual decision and they, the organisation and you as a supervisor get better results.

### This is my idea

The activity above also sheds some light on this next point. People can be awkward and difficult – not everyone, all the time – but they can be, especially when they face change. You can study this in more detail in the workbook *Managing People: Handling Change*. One of the key issues is whether they are involved in developing the ideas and the plans they are working on. It's what a senior supervisor in a food processing plant called the 'coffee machine syndrome'.

> *'You can see them round the coffee machine, telling each other why this new idea that 'they – management' have sent down the line won't work.*

*What they're really saying is that they're going to make sure it doesn't, just to prove the point that the managers don't know what they're talking about. The funny thing is that if you asked them what they thought, they'd probably invent the same idea as the one they're rubbishing.'*

Recognise this? Ever been guilty of doing it? Most people have and it's a symptom of a lack of commitment from the staff and a lack of respect from the managers and supervisors in some circumstances. It doesn't mean that you have to get consent for every idea and decision from the people who report to you – organisations are not democracies and supervisors are there to supervise and take decisions. But sometimes the smallest issues can grow out of all importance and clog up the normal effective work flow.

### The holiday rota

A supervisor in a printing works spent ages working on the rota for holidays. The machines had to be kept going and she worked hard to share out the time off as fairly as possible, using last year's rota as the model.

As soon as the rota went up on the board there were problems. Individuals came to her and said they couldn't do the weeks she had identified – they had family commitments, other priorities and so on. What they were telling her was clearly suspect, because it had worked the previous year. But she couldn't get it to work. Eventually, almost in despair she admitted to the staff that she couldn't get it to fit together and asked them to try and sort it out themselves, 'if they thought they could do better'.

They did. They always could have. They negotiated between themselves, sorted out each others' problems and presented the supervisor with a rota that worked.

They also presented her with some food for thought. In subsequent years the team sorted out the rota themselves, based on criteria she passed on to them about work flow, jobs in hand, schedules and so on. The staff felt more valued and the supervisor saved time and stress by not having to do the first draft or having to spend time trying to get it right a second time.

## Activity 1.4

Think about your role as a supervisor. In particular, think about situations like the one in the example above, where you work hard to sort out other people's problems and come up with workable solutions – only to find that it is difficult to get them accepted. List a few examples here.

Now look at your list and make a note of any where you could change your approach and pass on more responsibility to your people to sort it out.

*This activity may help provide evidence for Performance Criteria 5.2 (a), (b) (c) & (d) 5.1(a) and (e) in MCI Standards*

## Feedback

You may have found this a little uncomfortable – it means letting go of some control and this can be difficult. *Managing People: Leading from the Middle*, another workbook in the series, looks at this in some detail.

The simplest way of looking at this issue of commitment is to put yourself in the same position, thinking about situations where your boss does not let go of things that you could handle quite happily. The chances are that, when it's you in that position, you can identify how much your own commitment to an idea rises if it's your idea or one you have contributed to.

## Rowing in the same direction

Charles Handy, a writer and acknowledged expert on what makes organisations work, is a regular contributor to Thought for the Day on Radio 4. He told a story about teams one morning.

He said that he thought at first that a rowing eight – like the ones in the Oxford/Cambridge boat race – must have problems being in a team because:

- **apart from the coxswain (the person steering the boat) they all had their backs to the direction they want to go in**
- **they can't communicate properly as they're all looking at the back of the head in front.**

Then, he said, it dawned on him that they are an exceptionally effective team, especially because of the way they co-ordinate their actions. They each use their own oar at the same time, at the same rate and with the same degree of strength, with no need to argue about it.

In other words, they co-ordinate their actions to achieve a powerful effect. If only one of them got out of step there would be chaos, but it rarely happens.

## Co-ordination at work

Not that many years ago most workers in a car factory stood on an assembly line and did just their little bit of the process. They did not work together – each did his or her own small and separate job. They were quite like the management team in the example given earlier.

They didn't work with other people and they didn't need to have much idea what happened before they did their work, or what happened to the car afterwards. The result was patchy quality and poor motivation.

In the 1970s and 1980s factories like SAAB in Sweden led the way in team working. They had to overcome all sorts of problems, like personal bonus payments becoming team bonuses, flexible working and removing traditional demarcation lines. In the end they did it and gave teams of people bigger chunks of the work to do. The results were better.

The reasons include the fact that people co-ordinated their actions better with those around them. No longer isolated but working as a team meant they could plan work flow more efficiently, be more flexible and get more job satisfaction.

## Activity 1.5

Identify a team that reports to you and make some notes to describe:

**a   what its purpose is – what is it there to achieve**

**b   the separate tasks and issues it has to co-ordinate**

**c   how much control you have to apply and how much freedom you give it.**

*This activity may help provide evidence for Performance Criteria 5.2(a-e) in MCI Standards*

## Feedback

If you chose a team that, say, works on installing equipment in customers' premises or building something away from the work base, the picture is relatively clear. They get on with it, organise themselves and plan the job – dealing with problems as they arise.

However, if yours is a more difficult area in which to pin down examples, have a look at the following example and compare the principles with what you wrote.

The example is of a team going out to empty dustbins – apparently a simple task.

> **The Bin Men**
>
> A Channel 4 documentary called The Bin Men a few years ago, followed the workers of Westminster Council as they collected household refuse. A straightforward and routine job, but they had the freedom to:
>
> - be flexible and change the route halfway round, because of traffic problems
>
> - go home once the round was done – so-called 'task and finish'
>
> - handle complaints and unusual situations as they worked round, rather than call in the boss for every little issue
>
> - decide what was and what wasn't acceptable to be included in domestic refuse
>
> - report back to the manager on specific problems in their own and allied work (e.g. street sweeping)
>
> The control they worked under was broad. Their driver was the supervisor 'on site' but their senior supervisor back at base gave them the general framework within which they had to operate by, for instance:
>
> - clarifying their objectives with them
>
> - setting standards – such as health and safety, and procedures for dealing with scrap refrigerators – not to load them onto the truck but to issue leaflets about alternative arrangements to cope with CFCs
>
> - giving them up to date information on changes that affected their work, such as street demonstrations, road works and individual householders wanting one-off collections.
>
> Their performance made a complex process look simple. They were experienced and that came across as they showed the hallmarks of an effective team, co-ordinating the work under appropriate supervision.

## A sense of belonging

People work best if they feel valued and are engaged in creative activity. Someone once said that jobs were not designed to suit people – people have to fit into jobs. It can be a tight fit.

In the workbook *Managing People: Getting the Best From People* there is a more detailed study of what motivates individuals, but one of the key issues is the scope they have to plan and take responsibility for their own actions.

Creating effective working relationships is a two-way process and if there were a way for you to further encourage your people to:

- **increase their commitment to their colleagues, you and the organisation**
- **take more responsibility for and more pride in the quality of their own work**
- **reduce the number of trivial problems that get referred up to you**
- **get more job satisfaction**

wouldn't you adopt it?

One such approach is through teams.

## Activity 1.6

Think about two situations you are (or have been) in. One should be an occasion where you felt stifled at work, felt you were not being stretched and were bored with either the whole job or parts of it.

The other should be a challenging situation where you worked as part of a team – one where you had to think, solve problems and apply some creativity to the team's work.

What differences were there in what your employer and boss got out of you?

*This activity may help provide evidence for and understanding of Element 6.1 in MCI Standards*

## Feedback

This can be interesting. It's not unusual for the more fulfilling job to be more stressful, mean longer hours and even lower pay – but most people would still rather work in a successful team than slog away on their own. The results for the organisation are fairly obvious – better motivation makes better employees.

### Sausage Machines

Tom Peters is a management 'guru' who, in his books and seminars talks frequently of a sausage factory in the USA. He explains how front line workers are those classically seen as drones – making sausages is not a high-tech or a particularly prestigious job. But the company has record growth and profits, low staff turnover and virtually no disputes because, for example:

- they work in teams

- the teams are given responsibility for things way above their normal status – they put together investment proposals, and hire and fire their own people, for example

- the same teams visit suppliers and customers as part of a supplier/customer chain

- they plan and implement their own quality improvements

- anyone can go on any training programme, work-related or not, and the company pays.

Peters asked the top managers why they let all this happen. They freely admitted it was manipulative. They said that they knew making sausages is not exciting, so they encourage individuals to get as much job satisfaction as they can in other ways, through teams and training. The results show the success of the approach.

Supplier/customer chains appear in the workbooks *Managing People: Quality Management* and *Managing People: Managing Operations*.

We've looked at why teams are important and in the next section we look at what makes an effective team.

SECTION 2

# WHAT MAKES EFFECTIVE TEAMS?

In this section you will explore in detail the characteristics that make a truly effective team, but before you do you need to have a clear picture of the mechanics involved.

## The conditions needed for effective teams

You know already that teams don't just happen. They need certain resources and conditions if they are to work at all – let alone to maximum effect. One way of analysing this is to look outside the work situation and focus on other teams, say in the world of sport.

### Activity 2.1

Think about any sports team you are associated with, follow or know about.

List as many of the things needed for it to be successful as you can think of.

*This activity may help provide evidence for and understanding of Element 5.2 in MCI Standards*

### Feedback

Some of the things you wrote may include the need for a team to have:

- **the right number of players with proven skill and experience**

- **a mix of skills in attack, defence, bowling, batting, captaincy and so on**

- **team spirit – motivation**

- **a co-operative approach so they play as team members rather than individual stars**

- **adequate training facilities so they have the chance to learn or enhance skills, or plan set plays**
- **a committee providing support in administration and practical matters in the background to free them for their specialist endeavours**
- **an effective manager and/or coach, as the link between the hierarchy and the players**
- **a clear idea of what they have to achieve in the long term**
- **knowledge of the game plan, both collectively and individually**
- **a system for analysing previous performance and working out how to improve**
- **the right equipment and kit**
- **communication skills.**

There may well have been others in your list, but you can see from these examples that successful teams need all sorts of inputs. If only one or two are missing there is a real danger they can't perform.

The same sort of conditions that a sports team needs are needed by a team at work.

## Teams at work

In the introduction to 50 Activities for Teambuilding Mike Woodcock sets out the hallmarks of effective teams. He explains why teams matter when he says:

> *Organisations are essentially about people working together and yet so often they fail to capitalise upon the full potential of this. A team can accomplish much more than the sum of its individual members and yet frequently groups of people are seen to achieve less than could have been accomplished by the individual members working alone.*
>
> Woodcock, M. (1989) *The building blocks of effective teamwork. 50 Activities for Teambuilding*' Gower Publishing, Aldershot

This is a common theme amongst those who have studied the effectiveness of teams. Mike Woodcock details the key elements in an effective team which he sets out as:

1  having the right mix of people in the team with the right blend of skills

2  knowing what the objectives are – what they are there to achieve

3   a climate that encourages team members to express their opinions and feelings openly and honestly, without being shot down in flames for having their own ideas

4   a sense that they are still team members even when they are not together – they give support to each other and trust other members in the team

5   co-operation rather than inappropriate competition – everyone working on the same side

6   procedures that work – meetings, processes for taking decisions and so on

7   ensuring there are opportunities to stop and take stock of how the team is doing, individually and as an entity in its own right

8   relations with other teams and groups that avoid the fortress mentality and demonstrate that the team wants to be helped by and to help others

9   communication that works – in all directions inside and outside the team

10  the right sort of leadership – one that suits the team and helps maintain and develop all the other factors.

Clearly, your role is closely linked to the last of these. Developing teams and individuals means working hard to provide appropriate and effective leadership. The workbook *Managing People: Leading from the Middle* complements what you will see in this workbook.

## Activity 2.1

Look at the list above and think about the team you are most closely involved with – probably the one you lead as a supervisor.

Make some notes about each one and how well (or badly) you think the team is doing at present.

1

2

3

4

**5**

**6**

**7**

**8**

**9**

**10**

*This activity may help provide evidence for Performance Criteria 4.1(c) & (d) in MCI Standards*

## Feedback

What you wrote is going to be unique to your team, but it is an initial assessment and evaluation of the team's development needs.

It might be appropriate at some point – now if your team is already working effectively in most areas, especially those that depend on openness, honesty and trust – to ask them what they think about these same questions. For example, you may think they get the right sort of leadership from you, but they may just see things a little differently.

There is a simple but important maxim to consider here:

*Don't ask the questions if you don't want to hear the answers!*

If you prefer, save asking your team these questions until later, when you have looked in more detail at some further ways of developing teams.

Before you explore each of the issues in the list in the activity, there is a general point to think about. How big should the team be?

## Team size

In the activity on the sports team there was an issue about the right number of players.

You need to strike a balance between two competing factors:

1 the bigger the team, the wider the range of knowledge, experience and skill that people bring into it

2 the bigger the team, the harder it is for you to manage and lead, and the harder it is for everyone to find the space to play a truly effective part in the team.

There are some people who will always make an impact, either positively or just because they can't shut up. If there are also people in the team who stay quietly in the background, having too big a team will mean those people never get the chance – or are encouraged – to make a contribution that may be valuable. The loudest people are not always the most helpful, as you probably recognise.

A rule of thumb comes from studies done to find the 'critical mass' of a team – at what point does it's own weight make it break down and form into two teams? The general feeling is that this point is at about seven or eight members in a team at work. More than that and you may get factions starting to emerge.

## The right mix of skills

Without the right number of people and the right mix of skills you are in a sort of 'do not pass go' situation. All the other elements that make up a successful team are pointless if you are sitting there on your own or with the wrong people.

The individuals in your team were recruited because they match the specification needed to do the job, as you will see in *Managing People: The Recruitment and Selection Process*. Each one is skilled in the activities they carry out in their day to day work – technicians, craftspeople, clerical staff and so on.

## Technical skills and team skills are not the same

The skills people have to bring to a team are primarily about behaviour, how they operate as team members. It's almost like a job description for being a member of the team, as well as the one for their specialist job. You have seen this in Woodcock's characteristics of an effective team. They are not about specific job-related qualifications or technical skills – they are about team membership itself.

The *Institute of Management Foundation* in a module in the Competent Team Leader programme, sets out another, similar version of the characteristics of a successful team like this.

If you study this set you will find no clues as to what sort of job team members do.

### Control.

There is a sense of direction in how the team works. They don't spend much time going down dead ends and don't unnecessarily duplicate one another's efforts.

### Contribution.

Every team member is given and takes the opportunity to make his or her own particular contribution to the team's objectives.

### Respect.

Individual team members understand and respect the different types of contribution which their colleagues make. The extroverts do not shout the introverts down.

### Energy.

There is a 'buzz' about how the team works. Ideas flow. People work hard. There is a lot of informal, face to face communication.

### Reason.

Decisions are based on facts and discussion. Though team members have distinctive personalities, they don't use them as weapons in debate. Ideas are valued and brains respected.

### Achievements.

Good teams produce. Their quality is high. They meet their budgets. They achieve their deadlines.

Some of the points on this list result from team members' natural behaviour. But much of it stems from the ability of good teams – and good team leaders – to muster and deploy a range of different talents.

## The key issue

Perhaps the key feature of how teams work is the different roles which people play within them. Experience tells us that 'teams that work well', are more than the sum of their parts. One of the roles is clearly the one that you, as a supervisor, play in leading the team – and you will look at that later. For the rest of this section though, you will look at the roles you need members to play in your team.

### Activity 2.2

Think about your own team at work, What are the particular strengths of each individual in it? What, in particular, do they contribute to the team? For example, are certain people good at producing ideas? Is there someone you can count on to attend to detail – dotting all the 'i's and crossing all the 't's? Who are the active extroverts? And so on.

Don't spend too much time on this. You will return to it when we have been through some research based ideas about team roles.

**Team member**　　　　　　　　**Strengths: contribution to the team**

*This activity and the next may help provide evidence for all Performance Criteria in Element 4.1 especially (b) (c) and (d) in MCI Standards*

## Feedback

There has to be a mixture of strengths. The Cambridge psychologist R. Meredith Belbin and his colleagues have studied how teams work over many years. They have identified eight distinct roles which team members can play. Every one is needed to some degree in the team. If it is missing the team will not perform effectively.

The following detailed activity will let you identify the team role you play naturally and then develop the knowledge across the rest of your team. It will assist you in planning – and sharing – the team's development

## Activity 2.3

**A Self Perception Inventory**

(from the work of R Meredith Belbin)

This inventory was developed to give individuals a simple means of assessing their best team roles. You can try it yourself and it also is helpful in getting all the team members to look at their own roles, and accept others as part of a winning team.

**Directions**

There are seven sections in the inventory, or questionnaire. Each section contains eight sentences. Work through each section in turn.

For each section, you have ten points to distribute among the sentences which you think best describe your behaviour in a team situation. You distribute the points having considered your normal approach when you work in a team – the behaviour you tend to display naturally in a team situation.

What you do is spread the points to reflect the way each sentence reflects how you really feel about your performance in the team.

For each section, first read all the sentences and then decide how to allocate the ten points you have available. The points are likely to be distributed amongst a few or several sentences. In very extreme cases you might decide to give points to every sentence, or all ten points to a single sentence.

You must allocate ten points per section.

Write down the points in the boxes on the right.

Remember — there are no right or wrong answers, so please answer as honestly as you can. The value of the results will depend on the honesty of your responses.

## Section I

**What I believe I can contribute to a team:**

a  I think I can quickly see and take advantage of new opportunities.

b  I can work well with a very wide range of people.

c  Producing ideas is one of my natural assets.

d  My ability rests in being able to draw people out whenever I detect they have something of value to contribute to group objectives.

e  My capacity to follow through has much to do with my personal effectiveness.

f  I am ready to face temporary unpopularity if it leads to worthwhile results in the end.

g  I can usually sense what is realistic and likely to work.

h  I can offer a reasoned case for alternative courses of action without introducing bias or prejudice.

## Section II

**If I have a possible shortcoming in teamwork it could be that:**

a  I am not at ease unless meetings are well structured and controlled and generally well conducted.

b  I am inclined to be too generous towards others who have a valid viewpoint that has not been given a proper airing.

c  I have a tendency to talk too much once the group gets on to new ideas.

d  My objective outlook makes it difficult for me to join in readily and enthusiastically with colleagues.

e  I am sometimes seen as forceful and authoritarian if there is a need to get something done.

f  I find it difficult to lead from the front, perhaps because I am over-responsive to group atmosphere.

g  I am apt to get too caught up in ideas that occur to me and so lose track of what is happening

h  My colleagues tend to see me as worrying unnecessarily over detail and the possibility that things may go wrong.

## Section III

**When involved in a project with other people:**

a  I have an aptitude for influencing people without pressurising them.

b  My general vigilance prevents careless mistakes and omissions being made.

c  I am ready to press for action to make sure that the meeting does not waste time or lose sight of the main objective.

d  I can be counted on to contribute something original.

e  I am always ready to back a good suggestion in the common interest.

f  I am keen to look for the latest in new ideas and developments.

g  I believe my capacity for judgement can help to bring about the right decisions.

h  I can be relied upon to see that all essential work is organised.

## Section IV

**My characteristic approach to group work is that:**

a  I have a quiet interest in getting to know colleagues better.

b  I am not reluctant to challenge the views of others or to hold a minority view myself.

c  I can usually find a line of argument to refute unsound propositions.

d  I think I have a talent for making things work once a plan has to be put into operation.

e  I have a tendency to avoid the obvious and to come out with the unexpected.

f  I bring a touch of perfectionism to any job I undertake.

g  I am ready to make use of contacts outside the group itself.

h  While I am interested in all views, I have no hesitation in making up my mind once a decision has to be made.

## Section V

**I gain satisfaction in a job because:**

a  I enjoy analysing situations and weighing up all the possible choices.

b  I am interested in finding practical solutions to problems.

c  I like to feel I am fostering good working relationships

d  I can have a strong influence on decisions.

e  I can meet people who may have something new to offer.

f  I can get people to agree on a necessary course of action.

g  I feel in my element when I can give a task my full attention.

h  I like to find a field that stretches my imagination.

## Section VI

**If I am suddenly given a difficult task with limited time and unfamiliar people:**

a  I would feel like retiring to a corner to devise a way out of the impasse before developing a line.

b  I would be ready to work with the person who showed the most positive approach, even if they are difficult.

c  I would find some way of reducing the size of the task by establishing what different individuals might best contribute.

d  My natural sense of urgency would help to ensure that we did not fall behind schedule.

e  I believe I would keep cool and maintain my capacity to think straight.

f  I would retain a steadiness of purpose in spite of the pressures.

g  I would be prepared to take a positive lead if I felt the group was making no progress.

h  I would open up discussions with a view to stimulating new thoughts and getting something moving.

## Section VII

**With reference to the problems I am subject to when working in groups:**

a  I am apt to show my impatience with those who are obstructing progress.

b  Others may criticise me for being too analytical and insufficiently intuitive.

c  My desire to ensure that work is properly done can hold up proceedings.

d  I tend to get bored rather easily and rely on one or two stimulating members to spark me off.

e  I find it difficult to get started unless the goals are clear.

f  I am sometimes poor at explaining and clarifying complex points that occur to me.

g  I am conscious of demanding from others the things I cannot do myself.

h  I hesitate to get my points across when I run up against real opposition.

### Scoring

Simply transfer the points you allocated as you went through the questionnaire onto the first table below. The Section I scores go along the top line and so on.

|     | a | b | c | d | e | f | g | h |
|-----|---|---|---|---|---|---|---|---|
| I   |   |   |   |   |   |   |   |   |
| II  |   |   |   |   |   |   |   |   |
| III |   |   |   |   |   |   |   |   |
| IV  |   |   |   |   |   |   |   |   |
| V   |   |   |   |   |   |   |   |   |
| VI  |   |   |   |   |   |   |   |   |
| VII |   |   |   |   |   |   |   |   |

The following table is similar except it takes the sentences out of the previously random order. Put the score for each sentence in the appropriate square.

For example, the score you have given Section I, Sentence (g) goes in the top left box, that for II (h) goes in the extreme right hand box in line 2 and so on.

When you have done this, add up the scores in each vertical column and put the totals in the boxes.

| I | g | d | f | c | a | h | b | e |
|---|---|---|---|---|---|---|---|---|
| II | a | b | e | g | c | d | f | h |
| III | h | a | c | d | f | g | e | b |
| IV | d | h | b | e | g | c | a | f |
| V | b | f | d | h | e | a | c | g |
| VI | f | c | g | a | h | e | b | d |
| VII | e | g | a | f | d | b | h | c |
| Total | | | | | | | | |
| | CW | CO | SH | PL | RI | ME | TW | IM |

## What it all means

The highest score will indicate how best you can make your mark in a team. The next highest scores denote back-up team roles you could shift to if the team needs it and already has your top score somewhere else.

You may recognise not only your own behaviour, but also that of some colleagues. This helps you think about the different contribution they make.

The two lowest scores imply possible areas of weakness. But rather than attempting to reform in this area you may be better advised to seek a colleague with complementary strengths, who is naturally strong there.

The initials at the bottom of the second table represent eight team roles

**The eight roles are:**

**CO – Co-ordinator**

This is the type of person who excels at getting the best from other people, by recognising their strengths and co-ordinating their efforts. Good Co-ordinators keep the team focused on objectives. They are calm and unflappable, even to the point of being quite aloof on occasions. You are unlikely to see them leading the charge on a white horse and this is an advantage when a cool head is needed, but it can be a problem when the team needs a jolt of energy.

**SH – Shaper**

When a team needs shaking up, then a pushy, extrovert Shaper is just the person to do it. They can be uncomfortable people to work with (and for!), since they are never satisfied, can be aggressive to the point of bullying and like to get their own way. But team members will often forgive much of Shapers' behaviour because of the enthusiasm and energy which they throw into their work and generate in their colleagues.

**PL – Plant**

The Plant is the person who produces original ideas in the team. Plants can also be uncomfortable team members, but for a very different reason from the Shaper. Plants are often fairly introverted loners – not team players at all in fact. They are normally cleverer than the rest of the team, but may not be too practical. Naturally they are essential members of any team that has the slightest ambition to be creative (and these days that means every team at work – you cannot improve without ideas).

**ME – Monitor Evaluator**

Like the Plant, this is also a role for a thinker, but Monitor Evaluators have a different kind of intellectual ability. They are good at analysis. They examine ideas and, without taking sides or jumping to conclusions, identify their strengths and weaknesses. If you are leading the team, you will sometimes need to remind yourself of the importance of this role. It is very easy for a Plant to produce an idea which a Shaper leaps on with a cry of joy and proceeds to rush into action. Before you allow this to happen, don't ignore the Monitor Evaluators with their sometimes rather boring list of snags.

**RI – Resource Investigator**

Teams that are working really well can sometimes fall into the trap of becoming too inward-looking. The Resource Investigator will cure that tendency. These are the people who are never in the office. They are always out and about, meeting new people and collecting new ideas and information which they feed into the team. They are not particularly interested in detail or following up the ideas they come across, but, in a properly functioning team, someone else can do that.

### CW – Company Worker

Those who fill this role are hard-working, well organised, practical individuals, who delight in plans and systems. When, as often happens in teams, jobs come along that nobody wants to tackle, the Company Worker is the one who will pick them up. Don't look to Company Workers for a great deal of imagination or flair – that is not their strength. They are the ones who turn other people's ideas into action. This makes them very valuable since, as your experience will no doubt have taught you, ideas are often not hard to come by. It is getting them applied that is the difficult bit.

### IM – Implementer

As the description clearly implies, this role is filled by people who are perfectionists, obsessed with detail. When you need a job finished on time with all the loose ends tied up, involve the Implementer. As with the Company Worker, don't expect a lot of flamboyant creativity from the people. On the contrary, be prepared for a good deal of nit-picking from them. But if you want ideas turned into action, within a budget and to deadline, you need this role to be covered in your team.

### TW – Team Worker

Reading this list of very different roles, it has probably struck you that there is a lot of potential for conflict here. Shapers can squash Plants. Those who love systems and detail – the Company Workers and Implementers – and those who loath them – the Resource Investigators and Shapers – can drive one another mad with irritation. When that happens the team needs a Team Worker, someone who is conscious of and concerned about relationships within the team. They are the people who will cheer you up when work is getting you down – a kind of 'oil can' role. Team Workers keep the team functioning smoothly. Unfortunately for those who play this role, it is not very high profile, even to those within the team. The time when you really feel the need for this type of person is when you don't have one.

Before you started this activity you read that unless all the roles are in place, a team will not perform effectively. Why… and how do we know? Dr Belbin and his colleagues have studied this in a great deal of depth. Their most important conclusions are as follows:

### Balance

It is fairly obvious that teams which are significantly out of balance won't work very well.

As Belbin himself wrote:

> *What is needed are not necessarily well balanced individuals, but individuals who balance well with one another. In that way human frailties can be underpinned and strength used to full advantage.*

A team full of Plants, for example, will produce lots of ideas, but little action. A collection of Team Workers will be contented, but ineffectual… and a team of Shapers, while entertaining to watch (from a distance!), tend to create anarchy and, before too long, an explosion.

If you look back to the list of characteristics that the *Institute of Management Foundation* uses to describe how successful teams work, you will see how important it is that the roles are adequately covered.

- **Control is provided by the Co-ordinator who holds the ring, makes sure objectives are clear and pulls together everyone's efforts. To some extent the Monitor Evaluator also contributes to control by making sure that analysis precedes action.**
- **Contribution and respect are ensured by the co-ordinator and also, as a back-stop for people who feel themselves being side-lined, by the Team Worker, who is the sort of person who notices this kind of problem.**
- **Energy comes from the Shaper, who is impatient of apathy, and the Resource Investigator who brings more than a breath of fresh air from the world outside the team.**
- **Reason grows from the activities of the Plant and the Monitor Evaluator, with their complementary intellectual gifts.**
- **Achievement, the meeting of budgets and deadlines, the tying up of loose ends, rely on the solid hard work of the Company Worker and the Implementer.**

### Round pegs in round holes

Having individuals who are capable of playing a particular role is only the first step. They must also be allowed to exercise their talents.

Watch out for this if you are leading a team. Have you got the Resource Investigator tied to her desk doing routine work when she ought to be out meeting customers?

### A range of brain power

Dr Belbin experimented by putting together a team of very clever people to work on a business game during a training course. They were not successful. Later results revealed that a balance of intellect usually works best. The team members do not all have to be geniuses, a message which is reassuring for most of us.

### The right Plant

Teams need a source of ideas and, naturally enough, the ideas have to be the right sort. A brilliant microbiologist is unlikely to be much use to a team of social workers. The term 'Plant' is used because a 'sparky' person was planted in a fairly dull team to ginger it up… and it worked.

### An effective Co-ordinator

Harnessing and releasing the energies of a diverse group of people is difficult and essential task, fundamental to the development of a team. Managing the meetings and balancing potentially conflicting emotions needs a cool head and a calm approach.

### Flexibility

To some extent, this message is about tolerance. Once the team members realise how important diversity is, they become more appreciative of the contributions which their colleagues can make.

But there is another, very encouraging aspect to flexibility. Human beings are ingenious creatures. Once a team realises that it does not contain an individual who naturally fills one of the roles, they compensate. If there isn't a natural Resource Investigator, they set up a mechanism for analysing ideas. Even if they are missing a natural Plant, they can generate ideas by using techniques such as brainstorming.

## Making use of the information

Now you have this information – ideally covering all the members of your team – you need to work out what to do with it.

## Activity 2.3

In the light of the conclusions you have reached and the impressions you have formed, think about the roles you think each individual plays in your team.

To help you do so, focus on specific situations. For example:

- What are the best ideas your team has produced in the last few months?
- Where did they come from?
- If the team has been working on a project, what particular contributions have individuals made to it?
- Who is always on the phone or out of the office?
- Who loves detail?
- Who are the planners?

| Team members | The roles they play |
| --- | --- |
|   |   |

Are there any gaps in the make-up of the team? If so, what?

*This activity will help provide evidence for most performance Criteria in Unit 4 of MCI Standards, especially 4.1 (a) (b) (c) & (d), 4.2 (b) (c) & (d)*

## Feedback

The bottom line with this exploration of team roles is sharing it with team members – getting them involved in their own development. This starts with them recognising where their own needs.

The use of a technique such as Belbin's inventory helps to:

- **involve them in their own analysis of the team and its effectiveness**
- **get them talking about the processes behind their team working and raise the profile of the need for team development**
- **share with them the understanding and knowledge you have of what makes an effective team**
- **encourage team members to examine their own behaviour as individuals and plan modifications and improvements where appropriate**
- **accept the strengths of others, especially when those strengths would normally be at odds with their own natural approach.**

By doing these things it means that another of the characteristics of teams – review of how well the team is performing as a team – is being worked on. Indeed, many of the activities you do in this workbook could be used to open up discussions about the team's effectiveness.

# SECTION 3

# YOUR ROLE AS TEAM LEADER

In this section you will examine the role you play as the leader of the team.

One way of looking at it is through a checklist of all the things you have to consider. Have a look at such a checklist and then carry out the activity that follows.

## Team Leadership Checklist

An effective team leader knows and communicates:

- where they want to go and helps the team know by sharing a broad vision and clear objectives
- how the team can get to the objectives, through clear plans and an appropriate set of structures and procedures
- what each team member will contribute and achieve as their part of the overall plan
- how to handle problems quickly and decisively
- how they are going to monitor progress and handle changes to the plan if the need arises
- know where the strengths and weaknesses of the team lie, working to develop the strengths and overcome the weaknesses.

## Activity 3.1

Where do you think your own strengths and weaknesses lie in relation to the checklist? Make a note of any areas where you think you would benefit from some further skills and development.

*This activity may help provide evidence for all Performance Criteria in Unit 4 of MCI Standards*

## Feedback

Obviously, your own development is a personal matter for you, but knowing where your own strengths and weaknesses lie is the vital first step.

But it's not just what you do – it's how. The way you handle competing or different pressures and requirements is vital to your success and that of the team. Look first at how John Adair, who lectured on leadership and became a renowned expert in the field, described the situation. You may recognise the model from the workbook *Managing People*: *Leading from the Middle*.

## The three circles

There is a simple, powerful model which will help you identify what specific actions you and other team leaders like you should be taking as part of your leadership function at work. Adair's model shows three main areas which are not an either/or choice – you have to apply each one at the right time, in the right place and in the right way.

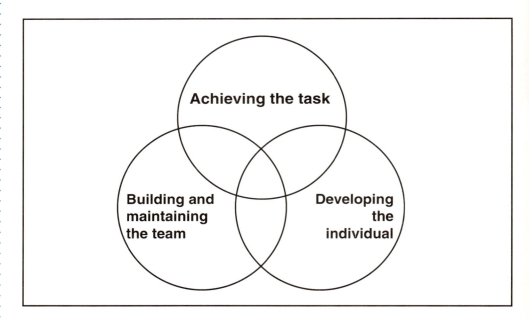

**Fig 1 Action Centered Leadership**

All the actions you take as a team leader cover at least one of these three broad areas of responsibility. Note the words 'at least'. Many of your actions will contribute to more than one area, which is why the circles in the model overlap.

## Activity 3.2

Look at the three circles.

Which one represents the role you are most comfortable playing, and why?

*This activity will help provide evidence and underpinning knowledge and understanding to support Unit 4 of MCI Standards.*

## Feedback

Unless you are very unusual you will have a preference for one... maybe two. The point is that they are all different sides to the same issue – you cannot get the task done unless you develop individuals and without looking after the team.

- **Achieving the task is the set of responsibilities which many supervisors think of first (some think of nothing else!).**

- **Maintaining the team means helping those who report to you to work together, as a team. This set of responsibilities may be easy to remember to tackle when, say, you and your team are all together in an open plan office. But when they are out on the road like a sales team or physically separated in a large retail outlet or factory or distribution depot, maintaining the team may prove more challenging.**

- **Supporting individuals begins with recognising that each individual is different from the next. They have different levels of knowledge, different skills, different personalities, different types of experience. This may occasionally prove awkward for you, but it is mostly very good news. What it implies for your role as a team leader is that you must understand and react to your people as individuals.**

## Activity 3.3

Think about as many of the specific activities that make up your day to day work with your team, as you can. Fit them into the three areas of responsibility – everything you do with your people should fit into one of the three. There are a couple of examples, to start you off.

| The three circles | Specific activities |
|---|---|
| Perform the task | e.g. Set production schedules for staff |
| Maintain the team | e.g. Holding a team meeting |
| Support Individuals | e.g. Giving someone feedback on their work |

*This activity may help provide evidence towards Performance Criteria 4.2 (b) (c) (d) & (e) in MCI Standards*

## Feedback

Naturally, what you do is fixed by your own situation, but the chances are you included ideas like the following:

Activities you might carry out to achieve a task include:

- **setting objectives**
- **monitoring and chasing progress**
- **issuing orders and instructions and progress reports.**

Activities you might carry out to maintain the team include:

- **delivering a briefing to your complete team**
- **reviewing progress with the team, both about the task and about the team's development**

- **getting together to solve problems that arise during work on the task.**

Activities you might carry out to develop the individual include:

- **arranging for a member of your team to go on a training course to address a particular weakness**
- **coaching someone at the workplace**
- **planned delegation to expose them to higher grade tasks.**

So Adair's model shows you have three sets of demands.

## Activity 3.4

Identify in your mind a team where you are not the leader but are a member.

How well does the leader of that team balance these three sets of demands?

Make some notes of specific examples to show where they do well, or less well.

**He/she is strong on...**                    **He/she is weak on...**

*This activity may help provide evidence towards all the Performance Criteria in Unit 5 in MCI Standards*

## Feedback

People learn most from experience. The point here is not to criticise someone else who may not have had the benefit of studying the dynamics of teams as you have – it is to transfer the analysis onto your own performance. The chances are you were doing this sub-consciously as you thought about the other team leader – thinking things like:

- **do I do that, too?**
- **at least I'm not like that**
- **I could learn a thing or two here.**

Ask yourself – how much am I like him/her? How much do I differ? What can I do to improve my weaknesses and build on my strengths?

### Sharing leadership

One of the key issues in team leadership – reflected in the MCI Standards – is the extent to which the whole team is involved in its own development and in managing its work.

You do not have to, and should not, try to do everything yourself.

## Who is the team leader?

The immediate answer might be… the person in charge, the one who has been given the responsibility in their job description by the organisation. So, you as supervisor are likely to be the one who initiates and manages team meetings. But it isn't always that simple.

Sometimes other leaders emerge, sometimes another individual needs to take over for a time.

It depends on the situation, and the confidence of the team leader to recognise the strengths within the team.

### Activity 3.5

Think about your team and its meetings. Make a note of situations where someone other than the 'highest ranking' has taken over as leader.

| Situation | Who took over | Why |
|---|---|---|
| | | |

*This activity may help provide evidence towards all the Performance Criteria in Element 5.1 in MCI Standards*

## Feedback

One area where this rarely happens, but might be beneficial, is in chairing meetings. The issue of formal status tends to lead always to the most senior person chairing team meetings... but is that always right?

Suppose you as the supervisor are the formal leader, but your team role analysis showed that your personal natural strength is in implementation. However it also shows that you are not a natural co-ordinator or shaper – both roles that are generally comfortable in the leadership role. Would it the best use of resources, would it get the best results if you were automatically to take the co-ordinating role, because you're in charge?

If you do, in that context, the team has a poor co-ordinator and loses out on implementation strengths. It's difficult to let go of control in a way that recognises this issue, but you might decide to try it sometime.

## Personal qualities - communication, openness and trust

The worst performing teams are often those where the communication is poor. The words might be clear enough, the objectives specific and the criteria for success unambiguous. But the way people treat each other and communicate can make or break the team's success.

### Activity 3.6

Think back to team situations you have been in in the past – where you were not entirely convinced that it really was working as a team based on what you know now. Make a note of any occasions when you felt like saying something, but didn't. Then, as honestly as you can, comment on why you didn't speak up.

*This activity may help provide evidence towards all the Performance Criteria in Element 6.1 in MCI Standards, especially (a) (b) (h) (i) and (j).*

## Feedback

We've all been there. Everyone has been in situations where they disagreed, felt unsure, confused or just plain angry… and said nothing.

Some common reasons are that people:

- **don't want to rock the boat**
- **worry that their colleagues will think their ideas are stupid**
- **worry they have missed the point and they are the only ones there who haven't worked it all out**
- **can't be bothered because they know no-one will listen anyway**
- **know that someone else will talk over them anyway, so it's not worth the bother**
- **don't want to disagree because they might be unpopular.**

These perfectly natural human emotions are often hard to admit – and failing to admit them gets in the way of the team and its success.

So, what can you as a supervisor do to stop this kind of clamming-up situation?

Remember the *Institute of Management Foundation* set of characteristics of an effective team? The bottom line was that they achieve results through four key factors:

### Contribution.

Every team member is given and takes the opportunity to make his or her own particular contribution to the team's objectives.

### Respect.

Individual team members understand and respect the different types of contribution which their colleagues make. The extroverts do not shout the introverts down.

### Energy.

There is a 'buzz' about how the team works. Ideas flow. People work hard. There is a lot of informal, face to face communication.

### Reason.

Decisions are based on facts and discussion. Though team members have distinctive personalities, they don't use them as weapons in debate. Ideas are valued and brains respected.

Your role as the leader of the team is to use the skills and personalities of the individual members constructively – avoiding situations where people don't want to speak by opening up the discussion and clarifying that everyone, in whatever role, has a positive contribution to make.

In the final section you will explore ways of developing the team. An essential starting point is to identify how it is doing now, so you can work on appropriate issues.

### Activity 3.7

Ideally, discuss with your team the four key issues repeated above. If this is impossible form an assessment of your own. Copy the list and give it to everyone and ask the question – how well do we do each of these things? Make sure the results of the discussion tell you whether there is any room for improvement in any of the four issues, and if so what it is.

| **Positive points** | **Room for improvement** |
|---|---|
| **Contribution** | |
| **Respect** | |
| **Energy** | |
| **Reason** | |

*This activity will help provide evidence for Performance Criteria 4.1(a-d) in MCI Standards*

## Feedback

This activity will have given you a starting point for your own team's development.

Move on now and look at the details of how to tackle it.

# SECTION 4

# DEVELOPING THE TEAM

There are three aspects to development covered in this section. The first looks at the way teams grow up and mature. The remaining two centre on:

- **establishing priorities and identifying objectives**
- **planning, implementing and reviewing the action needed.**

Growing up is not the same as growing – growth means getting bigger, growing up and development are about becoming more mature, more able to handle increasingly sophisticated ways of working.

## Planning team development

As with any other action to make a change or an improvement there are some clearly defined stages to the process:

- **identifying where you want to be**
- **working out where you are now**
- **identifying the areas where you need to take action**
- **prioritising them so you can start with the biggest areas of need**
- **defining some clear objectives to specify exactly what you are aiming for**
- **planning action to get you to the objectives**
- **taking the action**
- **reviewing how things are going and making adjustments to the plan.**

So the first step is to work out where you want to be. You could do this from the work you have done in the early parts of this workbook – describing:

- **what makes a successful team**
- **what characteristics, behaviour, roles and so on it should have.**

Now move and look at where your team is now.

## Stages in the development of a team

Organisations are increasingly using project teams to solve problems, and not just at the top of the hierarchical structure. You can study project management in the workbook *Managing Products and Services: Managing Projects*.

Because organisations are encouraging decision-making and project management further down, the chances are that you will find yourself setting up, or working in a team. It is likely to be one that has to develop quickly from a collection of individuals brought together to handle the issues into a smooth, well-oiled machine.

It will help if you understand how this process works. You know that teams don't start out as teams. They come together as strangers – maybe not total strangers, and it could be at work that you are in a team with individuals you have seen around, or had dealings with as representatives of different departments.

## Four stages

There are classically four distinct stages in a team's development. You will see a fifth, later, but the four listed here are in common use.

### Forming

At this early stage the group is definitely not a team. Some may be enthusiastic volunteers and others unwilling conscripts. Though they may know why they have all gathered together, that does not mean that they have, as yet, a shared objective. It is much more likely that they will have individual agendas, many of which will clash with one another. This sets the scene for the second stage...

### Storming

As the name suggests, this is a messy stage and may even involve some open conflict. The pushy members of the group may try to bulldoze their colleagues into doing things their way. The quiet ones may withdraw into their shells. The impatient ones may try to rush the group into action. There will certainly be some very different views expressed about what this gathering is all about and how it should work.

Your job as the leader during the storming stage is to encourage discussion, make sure that the passive members of the group contribute, highlight and resolve any disagreements, agree ground rules and prevent action being taken before everyone is pulling in the same direction.

## Norming

As the group begins to gel as a team it starts to develop systems and ways of working to an 'accepted' pattern of norms. Some of these norms are very formal and written. Others consist of much more informal routines developed through the growing experience of working together.

Some teams never progress beyond this 'norming' stage. If you want them to get past the rather mechanical, norming stage, how can you create opportunities for them to do so?

If you succeed, you will end up with that most satisfying of situations, a team which is...

## Performing

When you watch a top basketball team play, there are times when you seem to be witnessing some sort of miracle. The players seem to have eyes in the backs of their heads. Though the game moves at lightning speed, they all appear to know where their team mates are at any moment without looking.

That is an extreme example of a performing team at work. They reach that stage by continuous practice, by sharing and discussing what they are trying to do, by talking through their problems and working together on solutions and by recognising one another's' strengths and weaknesses, so that they play to the former and cover the latter.

## Activity 4.1

Identify two different teams you work with, one that is well-established and one that is fairly new. Make sure one of them is your main team at work.

Where does each one fit, alongside the four stages described above?

Give some examples to explain why you have said this.

*This activity provides underpinning knowledge and understanding for Unit 4 in MCI Standards and may help provide evidence towards Performance Criteria 4.1 (a) & (b) and 4.2 (b-d)*

## Feedback

It is likely that you spotted some differences in the two teams you chose, depending on:

- **how long they have been together**
- **how well they are being and have been developed actively by the team leader.**

The worst possible scenario is a team that has been around for ages and still can't seem to norm properly, as a result of poor development activity. It doesn't always happen on its own, remember, and even if it does it takes a lot longer to get a performing team if you don't work at it.

One result of doing this activity should be that you can locate your main work team in the appropriate place in the four stages. This gives you a picture of where you are, compared to where you want to be.

### The fifth stage

Add a fifth stage to your list – call it 'mourning'. It happens when the work of the team is done and it isn't needed any more. In these circumstances, have a wake and don't let the team grow old and tired – kill it off. Go out on a high.

Unfortunately, getting rid of teams does not always happen as often as they are set up. They just seem to drift on, even when the work is finished. It descends into the situation where you have a Monday morning team meeting… because it's Monday morning and for no other purpose.

This problem is far less likely to occur in a team where the development includes regular review, clear objectives and open communication. The imminent death of the team will be apparent to everyone and its successes can be celebrated.

## A new addition

There is one other point to think about here. A team may be performing brilliantly and suddenly a new member comes in. It is effectively now a new team. If the newcomer is a net addition to the team:

- **the make-up is different**
- **the skills are increased**
- **the size has changed**
- **there is someone else in the team playing their own role.**

If it is a replacement for someone else all the above still applies, but at the same time you have lost someone else, their skills and their contribution.

One way of handling this is to use one of the key elements in a team's success – carry out a review of how well it's doing – to pause and focus on the new team. In a way what you are doing is:

- **providing some induction training for the new member**
- **helping the existing members accept the newcomer**
- **carrying out one of the required tasks of the team leader - to trigger the review process.**

## Where you stand

So you know your team's stage of development. But even if yours is a high-performing team it cannot be left to stand still. There is always something that can be improved, some way of making the team even more successful in the way it operates.

But what are the specific issues you need to tackle? Well, you started to look at this at the end of the last section.

## Determining the priorities

Look back for a moment at Activity 3.6, where you started to look at where there is room for improvement under the headings of:

- **contribution – people's ability and opportunity to contribute, get involved and participate, including the way you operate as team leader**
- **respect – the way people listen to each other, accept them in their different roles, see each other as colleagues rather than opponents**
- **energy – creativity, new ideas and improvements, solutions to problems, pace, hard work and activity**
- **reason – discussion, logical approaches to each others' ideas, accepting that other people have brains, too, and they may just be right.**

The following activity is possibly going to take quite a bit of thought and time. It should provide you with the foundations on which to build and develop your team.

Before you start, put your feet up and reflect on the team. Recall as many examples as you can of how it works, and get a picture of where it is at present. If you need to, go back over any of the sections in this workbook to refresh your memory of what the main factors are in successful teams.

### Activity 4.2

First, think hard and carefully about examples of how the team operates and record specific points in the appropriate spaces on the grid on the next page.

Then collate those findings and produce some statements to go into the spaces on page 70.

*This activity may help provide evidence for all the Performance Criteria in Element 4.1 and 4.3 in MCI Standards*

|  | We must improve this | We really ought to work on this | It's alright ... but we'd benefit from improvement here | We're already doing well ... no work needed now |
|---|---|---|---|---|
| Contribution |  |  |  |  |
| Respect |  |  |  |  |
| Energy |  |  |  |  |
| Reason |  |  |  |  |

**The main strengths of the team are:**

**The main weaknesses are:**

**Its pressing and urgent development priorities are:**

**Other important but less urgent priorities are:**

**What we need specifically to achieve as a result of tackling these priorities is:**

*This activity may help provide evidence for all the Performance Criteria in Element 4.1 and 4.3 in MCI Standards*

## Feedback

What you have done is fine as far as it goes. You have a blueprint against which to set some objectives and plan the action. However, this is your opinion only at this stage.

The whole team will benefit from sharing in a process like this, not only as individuals but also as a separate team entity, where the members put into practice the four elements you have looked at. As an American writer, Marshall McLuhan said:

*'The medium is the message.'*

In other words, the process itself demonstrates that the elements are being taken seriously.

## Prioritising

In any situation as a supervisor you have to start with the issues of greatest importance and urgency. This is one of the aspects of time management that you will see in the workbook Managing People: *Managing Yourself*.

In the activity what you did was to set some priorities, either immediate or less pressing.

## Objectives

There are some characteristics of sound objectives that you will see described in other workbooks in the series, including Managing People: *Supervising for Results* where they are looked at in some detail.

The requirements are that an objective should be SMART, that is:

**S**pecific
**M**easurable
**A**chievable
**R**ealistic
**T**imed.

An example of an un-SMART objective would be:

*'We are going to improve our customer service.'*

It doesn't tell you what is going to change, how you can measure improvements or when its going to happen by. It may not even be realistic and you can't judge whether it's achievable because you don't know what you are trying to achieve.

### Activity 4.3

Before you go any further, look back at the objectives you put in the last activity and check whether they meet the SMART criteria. If necessary revise the objectives here.

*This activity may help provide evidence for Performance Criteria 4.1(a) & (f) and 4.2 (b) in MCI Standards*

### Feedback

If they do, you have produced some clear development objectives for your team. You can check your ideas by looking at the following short examples. If you need to do a bit more work on your objectives, go back and tidy them up again.

An example of a SMART objective is:

*'By next January we shall have completed printing all the new order systems for the sales force.'*

There can be no confusion about it because it is:

**S**pecific – completed printing

**M**easurable – all printed, printing is to be complete

**A**chievable – (unstated) but agreed with the printers

**R**ealistic – sensible, worthwhile and achievable

**T**imed – by next January.

# Planning the action

So, you know what you want to achieve and by when. You have your objectives. Now you have to organise some action. As the supervisor leading the team you have the central role in planning the action. The checklist in the last section focused on this.

## Your own performance

There are several potential areas where you as the leader can refine the points in the checklist and take specific steps to initiate the process of team development. They include:

- **using activities to help the team develop itself**
- **encouraging participation and involvement**
- **nipping unhelpful conflict in the bud**
- **encouraging informal discussion and communication between team members**
- **supporting contact, communication and co-operation with other teams**
- **observing and giving feedback on the behaviour of the team – identifying helpful or unhelpful norms**
- **leading assessments of the performance and success of the team.**

However, you also know that you don't do it alone – the team has to work with you as a team on its own development. It is a continuous process, rather than something that can be said to have been done, or completed.

## Specific strategies

Remember – this workbook looks at teams and their development. The one entitled *Managing People: Developing People* focuses on individuals, so here you are looking at ways of helping the whole team to make progress.

The difficulty is that there are no 'off the peg' solutions that suit all teams.

However, there are several possibilities you might find helpful. They are general strategic approaches rather than detailed prescriptions and your role is to identify how each one can be tailored to suit your needs.

Look at just two of the most widely used. They have in common the need to get everyone involved.

## Encouraging participation

This helps bring team members together to work on their own development and to solve problems.

You might decide to do one or more of the following.

- **Simply put in front of the rest of the team the team development objectives you have defined from your team roles analysis and the other activities in this workbook. Then work together to draw up a plan. In a performing team this can be quite an effective way to approach things.**

    **It will get some good ideas out and the process of sharing the planning reinforces the involvement and contribution elements of the equation.**

- **Discuss a real problem that concerns all the team. Try brainstorming to get a good range of ideas together and then come to a consensus on the way forward**

- **Use simple job design techniques – building on the lessons learnt from Saab and Volvo. As a supervisor you may not have the authority to make wholesale changes to work patterns but there are some lessons to be learnt from the principles.**

### Volvo

In the early 1960s Volvo introduced self-managed working teams. They moved away from individuals on the assembly line to small, self-contained work areas arranged in a hexagon pattern. This physical layout meant people could see each other and communicate face to face instead of along a line.

Teams worked in these areas, each team being 15—20 strong and responsible for everything that goes into the assembly of an entire sub-assembly. These included the engine, the electrical wiring and harnesses or the exhaust systems.

Because they were operating as true teams they had objectives, and as long as they met targets they were able to sort out for themselves who did what, in what order and when.

Output didn't increase massively, but absenteeism went right down, staff turnover dropped off and job satisfaction and quality went up.

## Activity 4.4

Identify a simple area of your team's work where a job re-design like this could work for you.

Make some outline plans for how you would go about setting it up.

*This activity may help provide evidence for Performance Criteria 4.1 (e), 4.2 (f) & (g), all those in Element 5.2 and for 6.1 (f) in MCI Standards*

## Feedback

What you selected will be something only you know about. However as well as the team's feelings and the way they operate you should also have identified issues that set the parameters they have to work within – issues like:

- **whether this arrangement makes the best use of resources**
- **whether you have clarified with the team exactly what their targets are**
- **whether their limits of responsibility and authority are clear**
- **the extent to which they might need guidance and help.**

In other words, you cannot just set a team off without looking at all the characteristics of the team and making sure that the framework is sound enough for them to take their work forward.

Your role as a supervisor is to put in place those elements of the teamworking framework that the rest of the team cannot work out for themselves.

In fact, the key to long term successful team development lies neither in what you decide they need, nor in delegation so huge that it amounts to abdication – it comes from the whole team, and that includes you.

However, if your team is still forming or norming it will need some sort of short term trigger, an intervention to help individuals develop themselves as team members and consequently move the team to a higher level of development.

### Team building activities and exercises

There are several books and sets of exercises produced that you can use with your team. One is the *50 Activities for Teambuilding* mentioned in the Recommended Reading list and cited earlier. There is also a section on teams in *Ready Made Activities for Developing Your Staff*, also listed in Recommended Reading. The basis of approaches in these and similar publications is…

*I hear and I forget. I see and I remember. I do and I understand.*

Anon.

As it says on the cover of Ready Made Activities:

*Designed to be run in small groups over a lunch-time or during half-day sessions involving larger teams, this flexible programme can be tailor-made to suit your own specific requirements.*

## Activity 4.5

Think about a course, workshop or seminar you have been on.

What were the approaches used that made the most impact on you? Look at the following short list and state how much they influenced you and why.

- **lectures**




- **full group discussion**

- **small group discussion and feedback to the full group**

- **problem-solving activities in small groups followed by feedback.**

*This activity may help provide evidence for Performance Criteria 4.1 (e) & (f) and all of Element 4.2 in MCI Standards*

## Feedback

The chances are that you found the later approaches in the list the ones that made the greatest impact – most people do.

This means that when you are planning development for your team you should work on areas where the greatest return comes from the minimum input – and that tends to be the problem-solving end.

## Implementation and review

In a workbook such as this it is impossible to look over your shoulder and tell you how to implement the right approach. The basic principles are all linked to a key word that appears time and again in the MCI Standards – the word is *appropriate*.

## Activity 4.6

How would you identify what was appropriate for your situation? What criteria would you apply? Give a few examples to illustrate your criteria.

*This activity may help provide evidence for Performance Criteria 4.1 (a-f), 4.2 (b) (f) & (g), 4.3 (f) and (g) 5.1 (e) and (f), 5.2 (a-e) in MCI Standards. It also should demonstrate all the criteria stated in 6.1*

## Feedback

Essentially, what you wrote will cover the three circles again – team, task and individual.

In other words it should cover points such as:

- **is it right for this team at its present state of development and expertise?**
- **is it my plan or ours – what is the level of commitment?**
- **what are the limits of responsibility that suit this organisation and this team?**
- **will it do what we need it to do as a process?**
- **is it a cost-effective approach in our circumstances?**
- **can we resource it properly in terms of people, materials and space?**
- **will it help us achieve our objectives?**
- **does it fit our organisation's way of doing things, and so help maintain links with other groups and teams?**

If there are satisfactory answers to all these points the relationship between you and your team will be enhanced even further.

### Looking back

While you can assess the answers to these questions beforehand the real test of whether the answers were positive comes afterwards, when you review what happened.

### Activity 4.7

Imagine you have observed and thought about your team's performance as they worked together to sort out a real problem at work. You are now preparing to review with them the way they operated – both as employees doing the organisation's work and as a team

Note down the points you need to watch in the way you lead the review – the behaviour and skills you want to use.

*This activity may help provide evidence for all Performance Criteria in Element 4.3 in MCI Standards and may also help with Element 5.3 (all).*

## *Feedback*

What you wrote should reflect the key issues set out in Element 4.3 of the Standards – issues like:

- **the assessment you made of their work performance should be valid and reliable – based on the team's own understanding of what they were trying to achieve, as clarified in your shared objectives**

- **the assessment of the team as a team should also be valid and reliable, based on their own understanding of where they are as a team and where they are aiming to be**

- **your feedback should be impartial – and you can only do this if you have built up the trust and honesty you looked at before when you explored what made a team effective**

- **the review should be a whole team review, using self-evaluation as well as your input – working as a team to develop the team.**

## The end of the cycle

Once you have reached the review stage you and the team will:

- identify what went well and what didn't
- identify why
- set new objectives
- plan new activities to get it better next time and to develop the team further

and so on.

In other words, it gets easier once it gets going. It's hard to undo the progress you have made.

# Summary

You have seen in this workbook that teams are not just groups – they have special characteristics and needs that you, as a supervisor, have to be aware of.

In particular you have looked at:

- the differences between teams and other sorts of group, based around working together for a common purpose
- the make-up of a team – it's size and the need for skills as a team player as well as an individual star
- the characteristics of successful teams, issues like:
    - shared objectives
    - a good blend of roles that adds up to more than the sum of the parts
    - sound leadership
    - open and honest communication
    - trust between the team members
- why teams matter to you, the team members and the organisation – what the benefits are and what teams can achieve that individuals cannot
- your role as both the supervisor and a member of the team, sometimes sharing the leadership and always working from the inside of the team, as an integral part of it
- how you have to balance three aspects of the job – the task, the individual and the team – and how each is an essential component that complements the others
- the key development issues for your team, and the stages that teams go through from forming to mourning
- the process the team needs you to lead it through, including:
    - identifying where you want to be
    - working out where you are now
    - identifying the areas where you need to take action
    - prioritising them so you can start with the biggest areas of need
    - defining some clear objectives to specify exactly what you are aiming for
    - planning action to get you to the objectives
    - taking the action

— reviewing how things are going and making adjustments to the plan.
- **how the whole process is a cycle that builds on success and can get you to your goals.**

You should also be able to evidence parts of the MCI Standards, in particular the following Elements in Unit 4.

> **Unit 4  Contribute to the training and development of teams, individuals and self to enhance performance**
>
> **Elements**
>
> 4.1   Contribute to Planning the Training and Development of Teams and Individuals
>
> 4.2   Contribute to Training and Development Activities for Teams and Individuals
>
> 4.3   Contribute to the Assessment of Teams and Individuals Against Training and Development Objectives

It also relates to elements in other Units, especially:

> 5.2   Organise Work and Assist in Evaluation of Work
>
> 6.1   Create and Enhance Productive Working Relationships With Colleagues and Those for Whom One has Supervisory Responsibility

# Recommended Reading

Belbin R.M.(1981) *Management Teams – why they succeed and fail*, Butterworth-Heinemann, Oxford.

Kanter, R.M.(1983) *The Change Masters*
Unwin Paperbacks. London.

*Managing People in Teams,* IM Foundation Competent Team Leader module.

Morris S. Willcocks G. and Knasel E. (1995) *How to Lead a Winning Team,*
Institute of Management Foundation,
Pitman Publishing, London.

Taylor D. and Bishop S. (1994) *Ready Made Activities for Developing Your Staff,*
IM Foundation, Pitman Publishing, London.

Thomson R.(1993) *Managing People,*
IM Foundation,
Butterworth-Heinemann, Oxford.

Willcocks G. and Morris S (1995) *Successful Teams in a Week,*
IM Foundation,
Hodder Headline, London.

Willcocks G. and Morris S (1995) **Successful Leadership in a Week,**
IM Foundation,
Hodder Headline, London.

Woodcock, M.(1989) *50 Activities for Teambuilding*
Gower Publishing, Aldershot

# About the audio cassettes

Audio is a useful learning medium and closely supports the text component of each workbook.

The cassettes:

- **add colour and texture to learning, reinforcing the process**
- **use real-life examples and interviews to help you see the material contained in the workpacks in context**
- **are highly flexible - you can use cassettes while driving, commuting, at home or at work**

Each cassette will:

- **feature a mix of case examples, mini-documentaries and edited interviews**
- **be lively and informal, lasting approximately 40 minutes**
- **use managers talking about their experiences, rather than being packed with academic theory.**

## GAIN NATIONAL QUALIFICATIONS

The Institute of Management is the leading professional organisation fo managers. Our efforts and resources are devoted to ensuring that all managers continually develop and achieve success.

We award national management qualifications, deliver programmes to achieve them and assess both individual managers and groups of managers against the national standards for management.

If you would like to talk to us about gaining a **National Vocational Qualification (NVQ) 3**, through Accreditation of Prior Learning (APL), please telephone the Business Development Unit on **01536 204222**. We can also provide information about the benefits of membership of the Institute.

Programmes of development and assessment, leading towards the **IM Certificate in Management** and **NVQ 4** and the **IM Diploma in Management** and **NVQ 5** are also available. Also available is The Competent Assessor leading to the **TDLB Award D32/33**. These programmes are designed to specifically meet the needs of organisations.

If you would like further details of the services the IM can offer, please telephone 01536 204222 or write to:

Institute of Management Foundation
Management House
Cottingham Rd
Corby
Northants
NN17 1TT

# Ordering Information

Please see page 5 for a full list of all the workbooks and cassettes available in this series. Workbooks and cassettes are available as complete modules, or separately.

These are distributed through a wide range of consultants and stockists. Alternatively, orders may be placed directly with publisher.

For a full list of our distributors, price and availability, please contact:

The Flexible Learning Unit
Pitman Publishing
128 Long Acre
London
WC2E 9AN
Tel: 0171 379 7383
Fax: 0171 240 5771


Credit card orders may be placed direct to our distribution centre at:

12-14 Slaidburn Crescent
Southport
Merseyside
PR9 9YF
Tel: 01704 26881
Fax: 01704 231970